NATURE'S
MYSTERIES

TORNADOES

JUDY MONROE PETERSON

Britannica
Educational Publishing

IN ASSOCIATION WITH

ROSEN
EDUCATIONAL SERVICES

Published in 2019 by Britannica Educational Publishing (a trademark of Encyclopædia Britannica, Inc.) in association with The Rosen Publishing Group, Inc.
29 East 21st Street, New York, NY 10010

Distributed exclusively by Rosen Publishing.
To see additional Britannica Educational Publishing titles, go to rosenpublishing.com.

First Edition

Britannica Educational Publishing
J.E. Luebering: Executive Director, Core Editorial
Mary Rose McCudden: Editor, Britannica Student Encyclopedia

Rosen Publishing
Kathy Kuhtz Campbell: Senior Editor
Michael Moy: Series Designer
Tahara Anderson: Book Layout
Cindy Reiman: Photography Manager
Sherri Jackson: Photo Researcher

Library of Congress Cataloging-in-Publication Data

Names: Peterson, Judy Monroe, author.
Title: Tornadoes / Judy Monroe Peterson.
Description: First edition. | New York: Britannica Educational Publishing, in association with Rosen Educational Services, 2019 | Series: Nature's mysteries | Audience: Grades 1–5. | Includes bibliographical references and index.
Identifiers: LCCN 2018010016| ISBN 9781508106647 (library bound) | ISBN 9781508106524 (pbk.) | ISBN 9781508106586 (6 pack)
Subjects: LCSH: Tornadoes—Juvenile literature.
Classification: LCC QC955.2 .P48 2018 | DDC 551.55/3—dc23
LC record available at https://lccn.loc.gov/2018010016

Manufactured in the United States of America

CONTENTS

TWISTERS

A tall tornado in the shape of a cone whips the dirt in a farm field.

Tornadoes, also called twisters, have terrified people throughout history. A tornado is a storm in which powerful spinning winds form a column of air that drops from a dark cloud to the ground. Tornado winds are the strongest on Earth. They can reach speeds of up to 300 miles (500 kilometers) per hour. Such violent winds can flatten buildings and whip heavy objects, like cars, into the air. However, most tornadoes are short-lived and may not cause much damage.

Today meteorologists know a lot about tornadoes. They can **predict** where and when a twister is likely to form. There are many things they do not know, however. They often cannot say when a tornado will touch the ground or what path it will take. Why only some thunderstorms produce tornadoes also remains a mystery. The more scientists learn about tornadoes, the better everyone can prepare for them and can deal with future twisters.

Meteorologists use various tools to help them see the path tornadoes followed and the debris they produced.

STORMY BEGINNINGS

It is important to learn about thunderstorms because some produce tornadoes. Thunderstorms include thick clouds, heavy rain or sometimes hail (small lumps of ice), lightning, thunder, and strong winds. Thunderstorms form when warm, moist air from Earth's surface quickly rises to cooler parts of the atmosphere. There the warm air cools, clouds form, and rain falls from the clouds. Meanwhile, the cooled air sinks toward the ground. This movement of air causes high winds.

Violent thunderstorms with thick, dark clouds can cover the sky for many miles.

Sometimes conditions are right for giant cumulonimbus clouds to form into a thunderstorm.

Cumulonimbus

clouds are the source of thunderstorms. Sometimes a fast updraft of warm air rises into a cumulonimbus cloud while a downdraft of cool air inside the cloud falls quickly. As the warm air and cool air mix, they begin to whirl and form a cell, or storm center, inside the thunderstorm. Tornadoes most often develop from strongly rotating cells called supercells.

LIFE OF A TORNADO

A tornado spins down from the base of rotating thunderclouds. The whirling column of water droplets looks like a cone, pillar, or tube. The column is called a funnel cloud or vortex. A vortex can be a few feet to hundreds of feet wide. It sucks up dirt and objects as it moves along the land.

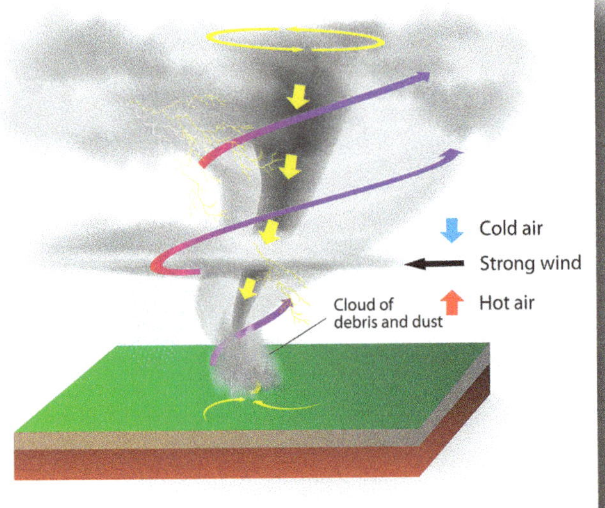

The rapidly spinning air inside a vortex acts like a suction tube when it hits the ground.

Once tornadoes touch ground, most move across the ground at around 10–20 miles (16–32 km) per hour. Twisters usually travel from west to east and take either a straight path or curved path. Winds in the funnel clouds turn to the left in the Northern Hemisphere and to the right in the Southern Hemisphere. Tornadoes often last only two or three minutes. Strong tornadoes can continue for fifteen or more minutes. Eventually, tornadoes lose energy and shrink back into the thunderclouds.

Tornadoes get their color from the dirt and debris they pick up.

TORNADOES IN THE UNITED STATES

T he United States reports about 1,200 twisters each year, far more than any other country. Most twisters occur in Tornado Alley, an area in the southern plains of the central United States, and in Florida. Tornado Alley includes the prairies, which range from west Texas northeast through the western and central portions of Oklahoma and Kansas and across most of Nebraska.

Dixie Alley also has many tornadoes every year. This Gulf Coast area runs from east Texas to central Florida.

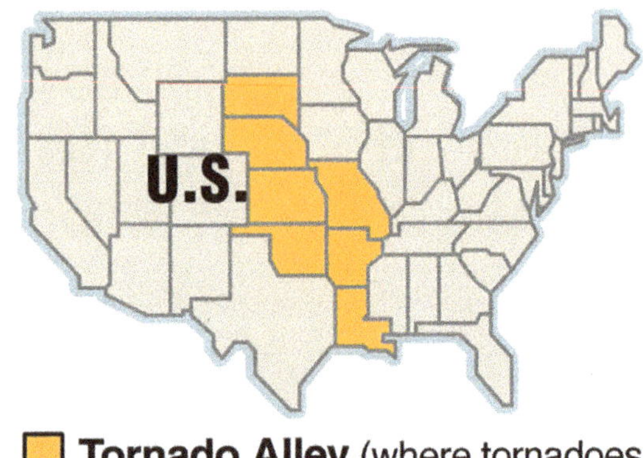

Tornado Alley covers a large section of the central United States.

Many storm systems develop in Tornado Alley, especially in late spring and early fall. Dry, cold air from Canada travels south during this time. Meanwhile, moist, warm air moves north from the Gulf of Mexico. Severe thunderstorms can occur when the cold air and warm air meet, creating supercells.

A pair of tornadoes takes a damaging path through the farms of northern Oklahoma.

TORNADO SEASON

Tornadoes can develop at almost any time of year. In the United States, they take place mostly in the spring and summer, from March through July. This is the time of year when temperatures increase and bring about great changes in wind patterns. The main months for the formation of twisters in the United States are April, May, and June.

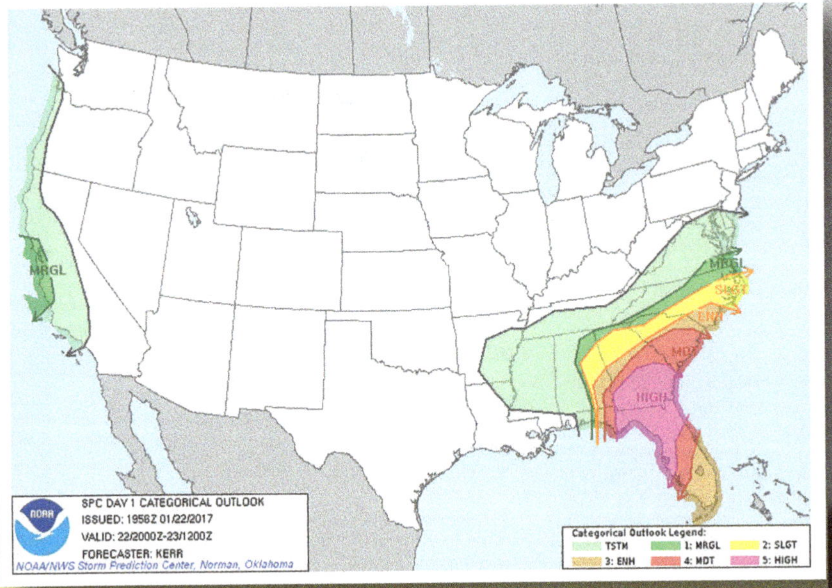

The National Weather Service predicted a high risk of tornadoes in northern Florida and southern Georgia early in 2017.

Twisters can occur all hours of the day and night if conditions are right. However, they are most likely to develop in the late afternoon and early evening. As the sun heats the ground during the day, the warm air rises. The air in the atmosphere cools later in the day. Severe thunderstorms can happen when the warm air and cool air mix, which may lead to tornadoes. Twisters might also form when hurricanes move onto land.

Tornadoes seldom occur at sunrise because the atmosphere is usually very stable at that time of day.

MEASURING TORNADOES

Meteorologists use different ways to figure out the diameter of a tornado's funnel and how far it travels and spins. The most important information they want to know is how quickly a twister rotates. The faster a tornado spins, the more dangerous it is. Scientists cannot directly measure the speed of a tornado. Instead, they estimate the speed based on the damage it brings about. The more harm a tornado causes on the ground, the greater its wind speed.

A tornado's strength changes along its path. The most extreme property damage usually occurs in a small area.

Tetsuya Theodore Fujita, a Japanese American scientist, developed the Fujita Scale in the 1970s. He used his scale to **classify** twisters into groups of wind speed based on how much damage was done to buildings and plant life. In 2007, the National Weather Service began using the Enhanced Fujita Scale (EF-Scale). This scale is similar to the original scale. However, it looks at more details of the damage caused by a tornado.

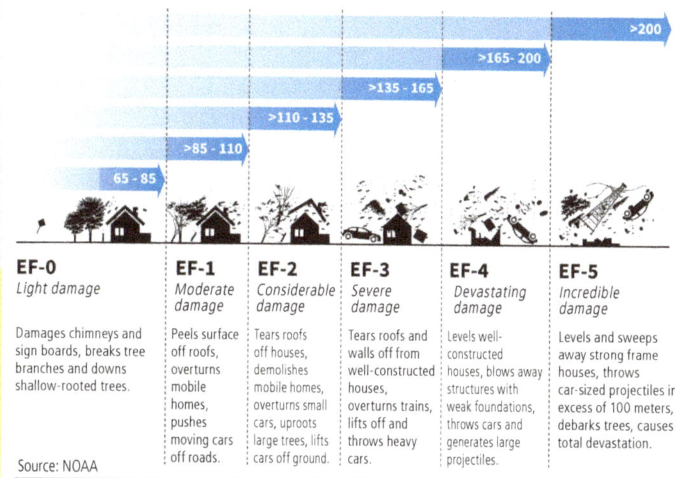

Enhanced Fujita scale for tornadoes

Introduced in 1971 and updated in 2007, the Enhanced Fujita scale (EF scale) rates the strength of tornadoes in the U.S. and Canada based on the damage they cause.

The three main classifications in the EF-Scale are weak, strong, and violent. Most tornadoes are classified as weak and cause few deaths. However, they can still cause damage. Weak tornadoes may break windows, overturn mobile homes, and break tree branches. Strong tornadoes make up about one-third of all tornadoes. They usually have a wide funnel cloud shaped like a column. The winds of strong tornadoes can uproot large trees, tear roofs off houses, and lift cars off the ground.

Only a very few tornadoes are violent. Unfortunately, they are

Some of the largest and most damaging tornadoes in history have measured more than a half-mile (805 meters) wide.

the most deadly. Such tornadoes can flatten houses and large buildings and throw animals, trucks, railroad cars, and other heavy objects into the air. The extremely powerful winds can cause broken glass and other debris to become dangerous flying objects that strike and injure people and animals.

In April 1998, a violent tornado near Atlanta, Georgia, destroyed homes, uprooted trees, and tore limbs off trees.

DETECTING TWISTERS

Meteorologists have several methods for studying tornadoes. Doppler radar is one of the best ways to detect and track powerful storms and tornadoes. Radar is a system that uses waves of energy to sense objects. Meteorologists study changes in thunderstorms with Doppler radar.

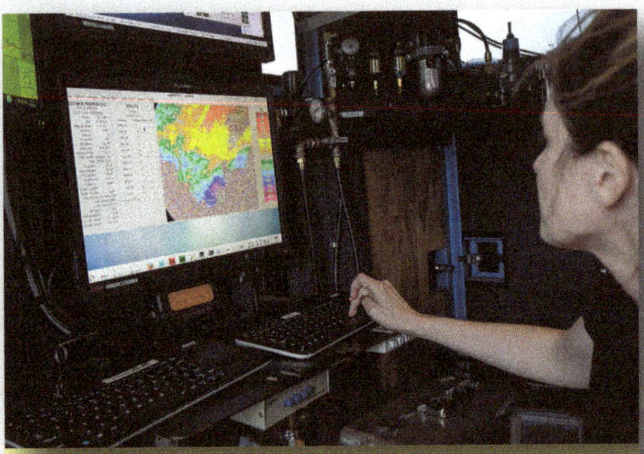

Doppler radar images of thunderstorms can show meteorologists where and when a tornado is forming.

Doppler radar measures the wind within thunderstorms. When the radar shows an intense rotation called the tornado vortex signature, it means a tornado may develop.

People called storm spotters report information about local dangerous storms and tornadoes to meteorologists. Spotters work near where they live, and the National Weather Service trains them. Storm chasers want to see tornadoes up close. Chasers include scientists, news reporters, or people who make movies or take photographs. They usually travel to places where tornadoes are likely to form. Storm chasing is often dangerous and not recommended.

The path of any tornado is unpredictable and can change instantly. This makes storm chasing very dangerous.

DEADLY TWISTERS

The deadliest tornado in American history was the Tri-State Tornado of 1925, also called the Great Tri-State Tornado. The monster tornado lasted about 3.5 hours and traveled 219 miles (352 km). It moved from southeastern Missouri through southern Illinois and into southwestern Indiana on March 18, 1925. When the twister finally lifted, 695 people were dead and more than 2,000 were injured. Thousands of homes, schools, and businesses were destroyed.

In 1925, the people in this Missouri town did not see the tornado coming because black clouds completely hid the giant twister.

During the three-day period of April 26–28, 2011, a huge **outbreak** of tornadoes hit parts of the southern, eastern, and central United States. Known as the Super Outbreak of 2011, it was the largest outbreak of tornadoes ever recorded. More than 300 twisters tore across fifteen states and caused at least 340 deaths. The outbreak caused billions of dollars' worth of damage.

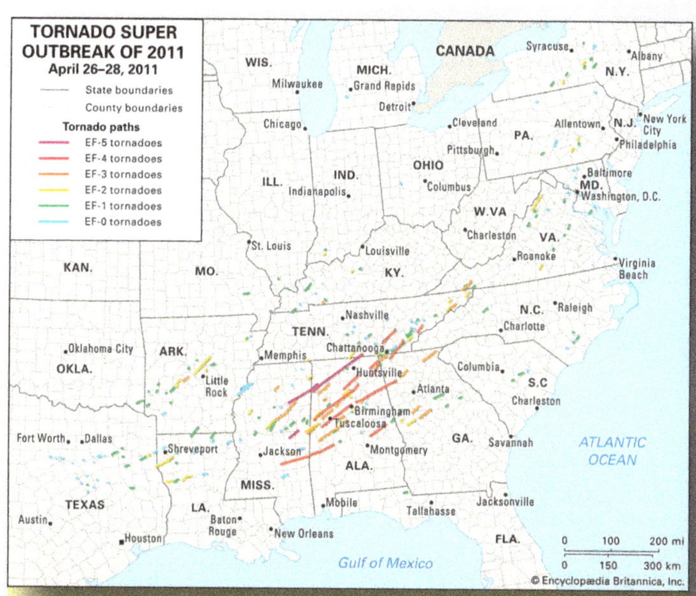

This map shows where every tornado touched down during the Super Outbreak of April 26–28, 2011.

WATERSPOUTS, WHIRLWINDS, AND DUST DEVILS

Waterspouts are columns of spinning air that touch and move over the surface of water. They often form in the tropics over warm ocean water. Waterspouts are usually produced by a fast growing cumulus cloud. They have been spotted in the Florida Keys more often than any other place in the world. Most develop between late spring and early fall and last five to ten minutes. Large waterspouts can continue for up to an hour.

The wind speeds of almost all waterspouts measure about the same as weak tornadoes.

A whirlwind is a small windstorm of rapidly rotating air that moves across land. Sometimes the winds can damage buildings and trees. Dust devils are a type of whirlwind. Most dust devils occur in large, open, flat deserts where the sun heats the air near the dry ground to a high temperature. The hot air spins as it rises into the atmosphere. People can usually see dust devils because the spinning air often carries sand and dust.

Dust devils are common in the Sahara, the largest desert in the world. The Sahara fills most of northern Africa.

LOOKING AHEAD

Meteorologists can often predict when and where severe storms and tornadoes might form. Sometimes predicting twisters can be tricky, because most tornadoes develop fast, touch down in a small area, and disappear in two or three minutes. Meteorologists use weather **satellites**, weather balloons, Doppler radar, and other tools to gather information to help them predict and warn people of dangerous storms that may produce tornadoes.

Storm researchers launch a weather balloon into a supercell thunderstorm where a tornado might be forming.

People can use radio, television, or the internet to keep aware of developing storms. The National Weather Service issues three types of tornado alerts to keep people safe. A tornado watch means that conditions are right for tornadoes to form. A tornado warning means a tornado has been spotted on the ground or on radar. In a tornado emergency, a severe tornado is ready to strike a town or city. People need to find safe shelter immediately.

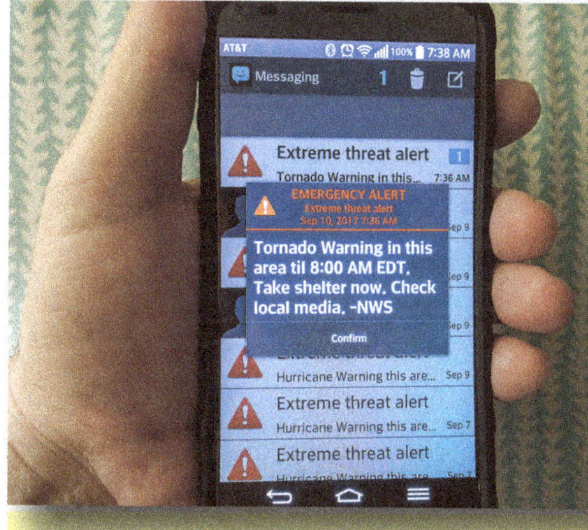

People can use a smartphone to get local tornado warnings issued by the National Weather Service.

TORNADO SMARTS

People need to take cover immediately when a tornado is nearby. The safest place is the middle of a basement away from windows, the lowest floor of a building, or an underground shelter, such as a storm cellar. It is important to move to an inside bedroom, closet, or bathroom and always stay away from windows. Window glass can break and fly around during a tornado.

Students are practicing a tornado drill. They are crouching in a safe place and covering their heads with school books.

A tornado may approach when people are outside walking, biking, or camping. If that happens, it is best to stay close to the ground, preferably in a ditch or another flat spot. People in such situations should lie down and cover their heads with their hands. Passengers in a car need to immediately get out of the stopped car and hurry to a sturdy building if there is one nearby. If there is no such building they should lie in a ditch on low, flat land. Hiding under a bridge or highway overpass is not safe during a tornado.

Some factories and towns provide tornado shelters for people to use during a tornado.

NEXT STEPS

Everyone should stay inside a home or shelter until a tornado passes. Local officials give updates on radio, television, or the internet. It is important to follow any instructions officials give out. People can text and use social media to contact family and friends. Flashlights, lanterns, battery radios, and smartphones are safe items to use in an emergency.

Everyone should prepare an emergency tornado kit of food, water, flashlights, batteries, a battery radio, and a first aid kit.

It is important to keep safe when moving around outside after a tornado passes. People need to call 911 for emergency help to report fires or if someone is injured. People must also watch for dangerous debris as they walk, and they should avoid fallen power lines. It is important to wear a long sleeve shirt, long pants, work gloves, and sturdy shoes or boots when cleaning up debris. Families may want to review their tornado safety plan to better prepare for the next twister.

Cleanup after a tornado is often hard work. Teams of people working together lower the chance of injury.

GLOSSARY

ATMOSPHERE The whole mass of air that surrounds Earth.

CELL The storm center of a thunderstorm.

CUMULUS CLOUD A type of thick puffy cloud that is rounded on top and has a flat base.

DEBRIS Pieces of something that has been broken or destroyed.

DIAMETER The distance across something circular, such as the funnel of a tornado.

DOPPLER RADAR A type of radar that shows the speed and direction of a moving object.

DOWNDRAFT A downward-moving current of air.

ESTIMATE To make a guess based on facts or knowledge.

FUNNEL Something that is shaped like a hollow cone with a tube extending from the point of origin.

HURRICANE A powerful tropical storm with very strong winds.

MEASURE To find out the size, length, or weight of something.

METEOROLOGISTS Scientists who study the weather.

RADAR A way of detecting objects at a distance by making radio waves bounce off of them.

SUPERCELL A strongly rotating cell inside a thunderstorm from which tornadoes sometimes develop.

TROPICS The hot, humid regions just north and south of the equator.

UPDRAFT A rising current of air.

VIOLENT A dangerous action caused by force.

VORTEX A spinning column of air.

WEATHER BALLOON A balloon with small instruments used to measure weather conditions high in the atmosphere.

Books

Krajnik, Elizabeth. *Twisted by Tornadoes* (Natural Disasters: How People Survive). New York, NY: PowerKids Press, 2018.

Murray, Julie. *Tornadoes.* Minneapolis, MN: Abdo Zoom, 2018.

Randolph, Joanne. *Tornado Alert!* (Weather Report). New York, NY: Enslow Publishing, 2018.

Schuh, Mari C. *Tornadoes.* New York, NY: Capstone Press, 2017.

Shofner, Melissa Raé. *Weather and Natural Disasters* (Spotlight on Earth Science). New York, NY: PowerKids Press, 2017.

Websites

National Geographic Kids

Tornado
https://kids.nationalgeographic.com /explore/science/tornado/#tornado .jpg

National Severe Storms Laboratory

Severe Weather 101—Tornadoes
https://www.nssl.noaa.gov/education /svrwx101/tornadoes/faq/

National Weather Service

Tornado Safety
http://www.nws.noaa.gov/os/tornado/

Ready Check

https://www.ready.gov/kids /know-the-facts/tornado

INDEX